with best wishes

Anudyuti Maitra

JLF-19

Anudyuti Maitra

Notion Press

Old No. 38, New No. 6
McNichols Road, Chetpet
Chennai - 600 031

First Published by Notion Press 2018
Copyright © Anudyuti Maitra 2018
All Rights Reserved.

ISBN 978-1-64249-183-8

A Touch of
Life

I DEDICATE THIS BOOK TO THE MEMORY OF
MY DEAR WIFE MUKTI @TUTU

Contents

Section C
Jaipur Literature Festival

Preface

Nineteen poems crafted by Anudyuti Maitra, the Artist of words, mingled with dash of sorrow some where and mostly with hope and love in their vista.

Each poem reflects a little wee bit of Anudyuti and takes the reader in a journey through his life.

His life walks forward despite the pain of loss of his dear wife and the reader can smell the happy odour of hope and joy of life in his poems. There are poems in which he stands dedicating his life to the will of God Almighty and love of God.

Nineteen poems giving you glimpses into the life and thoughts of Anudyuti. Poems of all colours, hues of life, as life keeps rolling on despite the motion of endless journey of Time.

Author of the Preface

Mrs. Aryama Sanyal

Airport Director, Indore

Section A
Theme of Life

A Touch of Life

Wondering alone,

    Bewildered

        In the Wilderness

As thoughts echoed

    Far Away

        In the distance.

Saw the light

    Sparkles

        And there she was!

Then I woke up

    From my dreams

        And she was gone.

Leaving me

    All alone

        Still Bewildered.

Music in Life

Music is my life
>Music is my soul

Music in the words
>As the seasons roll

Music for my love
>Music for the world

Music always to play
>As we grow old.

>>O! My Passion; O! MyLord
>>O! My lovely; O! My God
>>>Let me be the music.

As the seasons come
>As the seasons go

You are the only one
>In my life I know

Let your love be mine
>Let it always flow

Show it to me now
>Today and tomorrow.

Lord Advents

Christmas Time has come
    The Lord has come
The time has come
    Its time for fun.
Mary's gift to us
    Virgin child was thus
Mother's gift to us
    Lord advents for mass.
As Saints' beheld the child
    Bethlehem went wild
As the child cutely smiled
    With happiness, that was n't mild
Into the world for the love
    For spreading message like the dove
Happiness and love was the tryst
    Of the child Jesus Christ.

Ode to a Friend

Time gave me a blow
And made my life slow
Little did I know
That future will still glow.

Looking for someone
As life is still not done
Without you there's no fun
Time 'll still be on the run.

Searching here and there
For many things to share
To open my heart bare
Can you be that dare?

I know, you are not mine
Still for me it is fine
To me you are like the wine
As my thoughts and mind, drink & dine

Writing this for you

Which you never knew

Giving friendship its due

To make the relationship true.

Writing a Poem

Start writing a poem

      Without any reason

I know it is not a sin

      Nor any treason…

So keep on writing

      And try hard to rhyme

If you cannot

      It is not a crime.

This is written for you

      And no one has heard it

It is always true

      You can rhyme with a little grit.

East or West

As east goes to west

      With Knowledge at crest

Leaving Kurta for Vest

      In harmony and zest,

Our thought process is stressed

      With habits being messed

Though our ability is blessed

      But we are still obsessed.

This is my quest

      Will controversies come to rest?

As we go to west

      Though India is our nest.

What will be the test

      Is knowledge the best?

Or, is it only the west?

      When cultures are at fest.

Ode to Smule

Oh! What an app

> To sing through the Day

Listening to music

> And singing, all the way.

Creating ease of singing

> That's all I can say

As you sing to the tunes

> In the App, as it lay.

Delve into the music

> Follow the rhyme

Go through the lines

> And sing properly in time.

Upload it from the phone

> Then let it be known

To the world at large

> With Smule, without any splurge.

My Spiritual Guide

Ah! You are my spiritual guide
Always flowing in me like the tide.
By following You in my stride
You keep my life open and wide
Making my life an easy ride.

      Thus like, is my spiritual guide
      Whose principles I always abide
      While walking paths untested and tried
      With Him as my spiritual guide.

Oh You! My friend and my pride
You held my hand whenever I cried
Helped me to get my tears dried
As I lost my only friend my bride.

      Over grief, You let happiness glide
      Through Your principles as and when applied
      Removed my sorrow and all else aside
      Forever staying always by my side
      Oh! You are my true spiritual Guide.

Section B
She and Me

Happiness

Happy to be,

Once again free

Travelling with glee

Just you and me.

      You are in my mind

      Without any sort of bind

      Leaving the time behind

      As life's not so kind.

As you and I travel

Mysteries of life unravel

Treading over life in sequel

Munching sounds come from gravel.

      Thus I forget the past

      Grief is but so vast

      As time cures my heart really fast

      That's why I am happy at last.

Oh! Dear Departed

Oh! Thus was the life;

     Of my beautiful wife

Walking hand in hand

     O'er sea and land,

Sharing husband's time

     Making it really fine

Looking back we find

     A perfect and pure bind

Of body, soul and mind

     Leaving all else behind,

There's no relation of this kind

     For us, to walk through the grind.

She walked through the strife

     With husband all her life

And then came her time

     As she made her life sublime

As the time came

    For the Sweet dame

We put her to flame

    And over was her game.

You and Me

You are there

    Always for me

None does care

    As they cannot see

My thoughts which I share

    Whenever I'm free

With you my dear

    As and when it be.

There you are still

    Always with me

Walking o'er the hill

    Both in grief and glee

My thoughts and time you fill

    Even though none can see

Through the life's drill

    As a pure company.

Miss You

Oh! How I miss you,
>Can't you see?

Why did you depart?
>All so early

Here I'm all alone
>What can be

None to start my day with
>Is it destiny?

You were my best friend
>Now you are no more

I don't know where it'll end
>As life opens new door

I'm still looking for you
>Through futures in store

Please re-incarnate my life
>And bring me to fore.

Oh! How I miss you

        Can't you see

Why did you depart

        Without me

Now leaving me alone

        And truly free

You took away my World

        Like an enemy.

Life with You on This Stage

You were mine

Now you are gone

I'm still fine

But a little alone.

      This is life

      And all has to leave

      In this stage

      As the story of life, weave

Our time is bound

On this stage

As you come around

On my drama page.

Section C
Jaipur Literature Festival

The Jaipur Lit-Fest

The last day at the fest
Really it will be the best
When discussions are at its crest
And the Jaipur Lit-Fest comes to rest.

It will be time to bid adieu
After giving the fest its due
With remembrances quite a few
When going out at the exit queue.

Cute ladies running from here to there
With sylish legs both covered and bare
Moving around with speed like hare
As if life has nothing more to care.

The festival of discussions and style
With minds of participants so agile
As time and celebrations traverses a mile
Selective presentations are generated in a file.

Oh! The fest comes to rest

As ideas tingles minds to quest

Mixing views of both east and west

Jaipur Lit-Fest is always the best...

The Approaching Event

The approaching event
Where last year I went
Though I couldn't spend
Much time till the end.

Now eagerly waiting
Wishing to attend
The Jaipur Lit-Fest
From beginning to the end.

The festival touching lives
Of both husband and wives
Where, into literature, mind dives
As the festival, lives and thrives.

On the Third Day

My little girl, so cute and so small
Got the wind of the fest, in the hall
Started her first try, at the poems
Writing lines on paper, with real names.

That was it, she was so shy
Faltered to ask questions, as to why
The reading continued at boring pace
Quite unaware of the literary race.

So was her words, small and frail
Writings on the paper, in a trail.
A little girl, looking at fest with her eyes
That was the time, to leave, with tearful byes.

The Lit-Fest
and the English Ghazal

Oh! The crowd, looking for the words
Oh! The crowd, gazing at the bards
Oh! The crowd, Listening to the Ghazals
Oh! The crowd, Cheering public dazzles.

        That was the fest

        Is it the best?

The sound that was
The rhymes they made
The ghazals of the Divas
That reasons forbade
Ghazals and *radiff* thus
For public accolade.

        And that was it

        The entire bit.

Really is this the fest
You all know the best
In your daily quest
Thats the literary zest.

Festival Emotion

Oh! What emotion
Oh! The devotion
Oh! The words
Flying like the birds.

High was the passion of the poet
Who was reading together in a duet
Was reading her poems calmly
And observing the crowd warmly.

As one read, and the other looked through
Listening to poems, was all one could do
Whether liking or disliking, the words through
Striking the heart, for emotions to woo
Sitting on chairs, as if fixed with glue
That was nice, and too good to be true.

For Jhonny in Fest

Lit-Fest, the festival so grand
Brother and sister going hand in hand
Listening to poets, as we stand
Literary phrases from poetic bands.

    Enjoying the warmth of literary words
    Spoken Emotionally by the bards
    Flipping from tent to tent like cards
    That was Johnny standing by the gaurds.

Running around with camera in hand
Clicking at celebrities of all the brands
Listening to phrases and poetry, all so grand
Reading from books of different lands.

    The picture so great, the literature so rich
    Enticing the crowd, like the witch
    Repairing the minds, like the stitch
    Reciting words, without any glitch.

Thus was the emotional quotient of the fest
The Jaipur Literary Fest, at its best.